WHAT IS A PARLIAMENTARY GOVERNMENT?

KAREN LATCHANA KENNEY

Gareth Stevens
Publishing

Please visit our website, www.garethstevens.com. For a free color catalog of all our high-quality books, call toll free 1-800-542-2595 or fax 1-877-542-2596.

Library of Congress Cataloging-in-Publication Data

Kenney, Karen Latchana.
What is a parliamentary government? / Karen Latchana Kenney.
    pages cm.
Includes index.
ISBN 978-1-4824-0318-3 (pbk.)
ISBN 978-1-4824-3303-6 (6-pack)
ISBN 978-1-4824-0317-6 (library binding)
1. Legislative bodies—Juvenile literature. 2. Representative government and representation—Juvenile literature. I. Title.
JF511.K43 2014
328—dc23
                        2013028416
First Edition

Published in 2014 by
Gareth Stevens Publishing
111 East 14th Street, Suite 349
New York, NY 10003

© 2014 Gareth Stevens Publishing

Produced by Calcium, www.calciumcreative.co.uk
Designed by Keith Williams and Paul Myerscough
Edited by Sarah Eason

Photo credits: Cover: Shutterstock: Avella (left), Neftali (right). Inside: Dreamstime: Androniques 10, Aprescindere 35, Clivechilvers 28, Hypnocreative 40, Manonringuette 32, Pauws99 7, Petronella 5, Reddees 38, Res2500 30, Tektite 25, The guitar mann 11; Shutterstock: AlexanderZam 9, Anastasios71 6, Anyaivanova 16, Asianet-Pakistan 43, Gary Blakeley 44, ChinellatoPhoto 39, Dutourdumonde 31, Featureflash 20, Ferenz 17, David Fowler 23, 24, 26, Patricia Hofmeester 33, Georgios Kollidas 8, 45, Alexandra Lande 12, V. J. Matthew 22, Natursports 42, Anna Omelchenko 41, Lefteris Papaulakis 19, Pavel L Photo and Video 34, Dmitry Pistrov 29, Ribeiroantonio 1, 4, Rupa 36, Spirit of America 15, Sportsphotographer.eu 18, Vipflash 14; Wikimedia Commons: Shiny Things 37.

Printed in the United States of America

CPSIA compliance information: Batch # CW14GS: For further information contact Gareth Stevens, New York, New York at 1-800-542-2595.

Contents

CHAPTER ONE

What Is a Parliament?

The parliamentary system is one of the oldest forms of government. It evolved from ancient Greek democracies and monarchies, when kings and queens ruled kingdoms. The parliamentary system was very different from the single rule of a king or queen—it involved the people in the rule of their country. Today, it is a system that many countries have adopted and under which they also thrive.

UNDERSTANDING PARLIAMENTS

A parliamentary system of government is a democracy, just like the presidential system of the United States. A democracy is a type of government in which a country's people take part. They choose their leaders, and those leaders create laws to rule the country. Laws are the authority in a democracy. A country's laws, system of government, and protection of human rights are defined in its constitution.

In a presidential system, a president is the head of state and the head of government. In a parliamentary system, two different people have these roles. The head of state is the highest-ranked person in a country. The head of government is the chief executive, who is involved with making laws and running the country. The people of a country do not choose the head of government. This person is the leader of the political party that wins the election, after the people have voted.

The Palace of Westminster in London, England, is home to the two houses of parliament in the United Kingdom.

UNDERSTANDING BETTER

ARE TWO CHAMBERS BETTER THAN ONE?

A parliament can either be bicameral or unicameral. A bicameral system has two legislative, or law-making, chambers. A unicameral system has one legislative, or law-making, chamber. Canada has a bicameral system, with two legislative chambers: the senate and the House of Commons. Members elected by the people make up the House of Commons, while the head of state appoints senate members. What do you think are the advantages or disadvantages of having one versus two legislative chambers?

CONSTITUTIONAL MONARCHY OR REPUBLIC?

There are two types of parliamentary systems—a constitutional monarchy and a republic. In a constitutional monarchy, the head of state is a king or queen. In a republic, the head of state is a president. With both types, the head of state is a ceremonial role, meaning they represent the country at important ceremonies and in formal duties, such as meeting and entertaining leaders of other countries. Heads of state are not involved with the politics of a country.

The History of Parliaments

The ancient Greeks first developed democratic governments around 500 BC. This early form of democracy included three institutions—the assembly, which made decisions about war and foreign policy, a Council of Five Hundred, which made daily decisions about how to govern, and the courts, with juries of citizens, which upheld the law. This system survived for 200 years. It would not catch on in other countries until centuries later. The modern parliamentary system has very old roots, from late medieval times. It spread throughout Europe during this time.

THE WITAN

The modern parliamentary system has roots in the medieval period, which lasted from around 500 to 1500 AD. The very first parliament was the Althing, in Iceland, around 930. Even earlier than this, a parliamentary democracy began to form in England, which was not a united country at the time, but was made up of communities, or kingdoms, each with a ruling king. These kings sometimes held meetings with advisors and nobles. The meetings were called the Witan, which was a kind of assembly. The Witan discussed important matters that affected their communities.

Greek philosophers, such as Plato (below), helped to found democracy in ancient Greece.

Moot Hall in Aldeburgh, the United Kingdom, was built in the sixteenth century, and is still used for town council meetings.

THE GREAT COUNCIL

The king made the laws, but knew he needed the advice, and support, of community leaders to make the laws work. These advising groups became more permanent in the eleventh century, and after. A larger group of advising noblemen was known as the Great Council. They became the basis for the United Kingdom's House of Lords, which is one of the two legislative chambers in the parliament of the United Kingdom.

UNDERSTANDING BETTER

WHAT DOES PARLIAMENT MEAN?

The word "parliament" has French origins. It comes from the French word *parler*, which means, "to talk." After reading about the first parliament in the text, what does the word's meaning tell you? Why do you think that word was used as a name for the meeting of the two groups?

THE COUNTY COURT

For local matters, there was an assembly, called the moot. This was a meeting where local cases were heard and judgments made. Important local people, such as sheriffs, lords, bishops, and village representatives, heard the cases and made decisions. At this time, England began to be divided into areas called counties, so the moot later became known as the County Court. It was an early example of a locally represented government, and the basis for the legislative chamber, called the House of Commons.

These two groups, the Great Council and the County Courts, began to meet together in the thirteenth century. This was the first English parliament—a meeting of the lords, noblemen, and the representatives of local people.

The First English Parliaments

The early kingdoms of England later joined together with one ruling king. The first gatherings of nobles and local representatives did not happen regularly, only when the king called upon the groups to meet. The king also did not legally have to do anything that was discussed at the meetings. Unhappy with this, the lords forced the king to agree to the Magna Carta (meaning Great Charter), in 1215. This document became very important to the development of modern democracies. It listed the rights of the people and forced the king to listen to and follow the lords' advice.

A MODEL PARLIAMENT

In 1275, the first parliament was held that included elected representatives from each county, and city or town. The next such meeting, known as the Model Parliament, was held in 1295. The system continued to develop into the next century, and from January 1327 onward, the parliament always included elected representatives. The government of England had formed into three bodies: monarch, lords, and the commons.

These three bodies would develop into the current parliamentary system in the United Kingdom. This system of government did not remain only in the United Kingdom, however.

King Edward I issued later versions of the Magna Carta, the last in 1297, which is still in effect under UK law.

UNDERSTANDING BETTER

MAGNA CARTA AND THE BILL OF RIGHTS

The Magna Carta is very important to democratic governments around the world. It was one of the first documents that defined the rights of a country's people. Here is a quote from the Magna Carta:

"No freeman shall be taken, imprisoned, disseised [have their land stolen], outlawed, banished, or in any way destroyed, nor will We [the king] proceed against or prosecute him, except by the lawful judgment of his peers and by the law of the land."

Compare this with a quote from the US Bill of Rights, which was inspired by the Magna Carta: "No person shall …be deprived of life, liberty, or property, without due process of law."

Consider how these quotes are similar and how they are different. Does reading a quote from the Magna Carta help you understand why it was important in establishing the parliamentary system in the United Kingdom? If so, how?

The United States celebrated the 750th anniversary of the Magna Carta, the basis for US law, by issuing a special stamp in 1965.

European Parliaments

England's parliament is just one example of the development of parliamentary governments in Europe. Similar systems have grown in many other European countries. Sweden's parliament was established in 1809, and, soon after, the Netherlands, Norway, Denmark, and Belgium, and other northern and western European nations had a parliamentary system. Today, 18 countries in this part of the world have parliamentary forms of government.

UNDERSTANDING BETTER

CHOOSING A SYSTEM OF GOVERNMENT

The British Empire may not exist anymore, but many former colonies, which are now called Commonwealth countries, have adopted a parliamentary system based on the Westminster model. Why do you think these countries have this system of government? How do you think the British Empire helped spread this system around the world?

The UK parliamentary system is named the Westminster model, because its parliament is housed in the Palace of Westminster.

PEOPLE'S REPRESENTATION

Although the different parliaments across Europe developed in their own ways, they eventually included representation of people from different social and economic classes. These parliaments also marked a change from a monarch's complete power over government. Where there was a parliament, a monarch had to make decisions with the people of the country they ruled.

The parliamentary system that developed in England, and later the United Kingdom, was the system that many countries adopted. It is called the Westminster system.

During a British celebration of the rule of Queen Elizabeth II, members of a boat team held the flags of the Commonwealth countries.

UNDERSTANDING BETTER

THE BRITISH COMMONWEALTH

The United Kingdom once had a much larger world influence during the time of the British Empire, which lasted from around the seventeenth to the twentieth centuries. The empire had settlements and colonies in many parts of the world, including Africa, the Caribbean, Asia, and the colonies of America.

Some countries, such as Ireland and America, gained their independence from the British Empire through wars. Other countries, such as Canada, Australia, and New Zealand, became independent nations, but kept ties with the United Kingdom. They later formed part of the British Commonwealth. Although they are independent nations, they have kept ties with the United Kingdom, and have also kept the British monarchy as their head of state.

World Parliaments

While there are many countries throughout Europe that have a parliamentary system of government, other parts of the world have also adopted this system. Today, 56 countries have a parliamentary democracy, meaning it is the second most common form of government. Of those 56 countries, 31 are constitutional monarchies and 25 are republics. Japan also has a parliamentary system, with its head of state being the emperor of Japan.

AFRICA, ASIA, AND OCEANIA

Many African and Asian countries have adopted the parliamentary system. Lesotho and Mauritius, two former British colonies in Africa, use that system of government, as does Ethiopia. India, once part of the British Empire, introduced a parliamentary system in 1947. It has a president as head of state, a prime minister as head of government, and two legislative houses: the Rajya Sabha (Council of States) and Lok Sabha (House of the People). Thailand established a parliament in 1992. Japan also has a parliamentary system, established in 1946. Australia, New Zealand, and Papua New Guinea also have parliamentary systems. New Zealand's formed in 1853, Australia's in 1901, and Papua New Guinea's as recently as 1975.

India's government buildings are located in New Delhi.

THE AMERICAS AND THE CARIBBEAN

Canada established its parliamentary system in 1867. In the Caribbean and Central America, 11 countries also have parliaments, including Antigua, Bahamas, Barbados, Dominica, and Jamaica. All these countries are part of the British Commonwealth and adopted the Westminster system when they became independent nations.

Parliamentary governments have been established around the world, governing one-third of the world's population. From its roots in the United Kingdom to the world, the parliamentary system remains a governmental system that works for many countries.

UNDERSTANDING BETTER

MAPPING PARLIAMENTS

Take a look at the map below. It shows the countries that have parliamentary systems of government. After reading about how parliamentary governments have spread around the world, what information does the map tell you? Does it help you understand the text?

KEY

▮ Constitutional monarchies
▯ Parliamentary republics where parliaments are effectively supreme over a separate head of state
▯ Parliamentary republics with an executive president elected by and responsible to a parliament

CHAPTER TWO

Inside a Parliament

Different parliaments around the world vary in how they operate. These differences have developed according to the history and needs of each country. All countries that have a parliament have assemblies of representatives and executive branches. There are three defining characteristics of all parliamentary systems: head of state, head of government, and executive branch.

In Germany, former federal president, Christian Wulff, received Pope Benedict XVI as part of his head of state duties.

HEAD OF STATE

The role of this position is separate from that of the head of government. The head of state is a patriotic and ceremonial representative of the country. This person may be the most important in the whole country, but they do not have power to make political decisions. The head of state can be a president or a monarch.

HEAD OF GOVERNMENT

The head of state appoints the head of government. The head of government is the leader of the political party that has the most support in the main assembly once the members of that assembly have been voted in during an election. The head of government forms the government by choosing a group of trusted advisors, known as a cabinet, from other members of parliament. This group forms the executive branch.

UNDERSTANDING BETTER

MONARCHS VERSUS PRESIDENTS

A monarch is a king or queen, who passes the title down through their family. A parliamentary republic does not have a monarch as its head of state. Instead, a president fills this role. The people of a country with a monarch have no say in choosing that person, but the people of a republic can elect their president. While parliaments may change every few years, monarchs remain in their roles, sometimes for decades. What do you think is the advantage of having a monarch as the head of state? What do you think is the advantage of having a president as the head of state?

EXECUTIVE BRANCH

The people who make up the executive branch are chosen from members of the assembly. They are the top leaders of the government and have the job of drawing up, and implementing, the changes and laws that they want to make. They are responsible to and need the support of the assembly.

We will take a look at the defining structure of the UK parliament to understand better how a parliamentary government works.

British monarch, Queen Elizabeth II, met with US president, George Bush, in 2007.

The UK Parliament System

Just like other democratic bodies, parliaments are arranged so that there is a division of power between different groups of people. This ensures that no one branch of government has too much power over a country. The UK parliament is made up of three branches: the executive (the people who make the government), the legislature (parliament itself), and the judiciary (the courts).

UNDERSTANDING BETTER

PALACE FOR PARLIAMENT

Look at the image of the Palace of Westminster below. This building was once a residence, but became the home of parliament in the late medieval period. Why do you think this palace was chosen for the parliament?

THE EXECUTIVE

This branch contains the monarch, the prime minister (the head of government), the cabinet, and all those who serve and support the government, called civil servants. The prime minister chooses 20 or more trusted advisors (also called ministers or secretaries) to form the cabinet, taken from members of the

The Palace of Westminster is a hugely impressive building with intricately carved stonework and wonderful monuments, such as this statue of King Richard I of England.

two legislative bodies, the House of Commons and the House of Lords. Together, they all form the government, whose job it is to run a country according to its existing laws and to propose new laws.

THE LEGISLATURE

The UK parliament has a bicameral structure. Its two legislative bodies are the House of Commons and the House of Lords. The Commons contains more than 600 members, who are elected by the public. The Lords has more than 700 members, appointed by the head of state. Together, they form the legislature, which means they make laws, examine the actions of the government, and debate, or talk through, issues that are important to the country.

The Middlesex Guildhall is home to the UK Supreme Court.

THE JUDICIARY

This branch is made up of the courts of the United Kingdom, and includes the Supreme Court, the Court of Appeal, the High Court, and the Regional and District Courts. This branch judges whether the laws of the country are just and being appropriately followed by the people.

A parliamentary government is a democracy. This means that the government is ruled by its people. Citizens of the country elect representatives during elections. The elected officials represent the people of a certain area of the country in meetings of parliament. They vote for or against laws on behalf of the people

they represent. A constitution is a document that sets out the rules of governing a country. A parliamentary democracy is based upon its country's constitution. The British Constitution's origins date back to around 1066. It is an evolving document. It was meant to be amended and has changed throughout the centuries. These changes are made through Acts of Parliament.

The role of parliament is to make laws, represent the people, and analyze the work of the government. This work of the UK parliament is done in the Palace of Westminster.

The Backbone of Democracy

A parliamentary democracy is based on its country's constitution, which sets out the rules of governing that country and the function of the government. It defines where certain powers lie within a country, how they are constructed, and how they operate. It also defines the rights of a country's people. A constitution does not set out how the government works in a practical way, however. Those working systems evolve in each government.

Once the leader of the Conservative Party, David Cameron (left) became prime minister in 2010.

THE CONSTITUTION

In the United Kingdom, the constitution dates back to around 1066, when the Normans invaded and conquered England. It is an evolving set of rules. Unlike the United States, the United Kingdom does not have this set out in an actual document, but has what is sometimes called an "unwritten constitution." For example, it is not written anywhere that the prime minister has to be chosen from the House of Commons. Yet, this has become common practice in the United Kingdom government. Most younger countries have written constitutions. This is because one had to be created when the country was formed.

THE RULE OF LAW

Originating in the political world of ancient Greece, the "rule of law" is a very old principle of great importance to the UK Constitution.

UNDERSTANDING BETTER

CONSTITUTIONS AND PEOPLE'S RIGHTS

"A constitution is not the act of a government, but of a people constituting a government; and government without a constitution, is power without a right."

These words were written in 1795 by Thomas Paine, one of the founding fathers of the United States, in his book *The Rights of Man*. He often spoke about the rights of a country's people. Read Paine's quote above. What do you think it means?

It means that no one is above the law of a country, which is a basic principle of most civilized societies. It signifies, too, that a country's people, its rulers, and its government are all subject to the laws of that country. A parliament is expected to observe the rule of law as part of the democratic process.

Executive Powers

A prime minister is the chief executive power in a parliamentary system. Instead of being directly elected by the people, as a president is, a prime minister is chosen from the members of the elected legislature. One party usually has the majority in the legislature, and the leader of that party will be the prime minister, as well as serving as an elected member of parliament.

WHAT IS THE PRIME MINISTER RESPONSIBLE FOR?

A prime minister oversees the laws proposed by the government and passed by parliament, appoints judges and other government posts, and is responsible for all the agencies and civil servants who run the affairs of government. In the United Kingdom, the prime minister regularly meets with the monarch, who is allowed to express his or her own views and give advice, but must not try to influence how the government acts.

The prime minister is actively involved with the business of the legislature. During parliamentary sessions, this involves making formal announcements, answering questions from members of parliament, and taking part in debates. These duties are also shared with the cabinet, which helps the prime minister make government decisions.

The UK prime minister's office is located at 10 Downing Street, in London. Here, prime minister David Cameron greets US president Barack Obama and his wife, Michelle, outside his office.

NO CONFIDENCE

The prime minister is accountable to the UK parliament and needs the support of the majority of its members. If members of parliament have serious doubts about the current prime minister and the government, the members can cast a vote of "no confidence." If, after 14 days, the parliament still has no confidence in the government, a general, or national, election is held to form a new government.

This diagram shows how parliamentary and presidential executives come to power.

Presidential and Parliamentary Governments

The presidential voters elect the legislature and the chief executive, who is part of the executive branch. The legislature and executive are independent and coequal.

The parliamentary voters elect the legislature. The chief executive is drawn from the legislature.

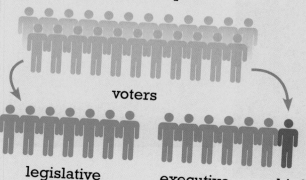

voters

legislative branch

executive branch

chief executive

voters

legislative branch

chief executive

The Cabinet

At the center of the UK government is the cabinet. The cabinet is made up of ministers chosen by the prime minister from members of parliament. There are around 20 ministers in the UK cabinet. They are senior members of the government who meet weekly with the prime minister to discuss important issues.

DEPARTMENTS AND AGENCIES

The prime minister also chooses people to head up departments and agencies of the government, such as the Department for Education. There are around 100 ministers who are responsible for more than 40 departments. Government employees, called civil servants, do the day-to-day running of the departments, but it is the ministers who make sure policies are properly carried out.

In the UK government there are more than 300 agencies and other public bodies that need to be run. Not all of these departments, agencies, and public bodies are run by ministers, though—civil servants run some.

DEPUTY PRIME MINISTER

Also supporting the prime minister is a deputy prime minister. This person may head different committees in the government and help build relationships with other countries. The deputy prime minister can also take over the prime minister's role, if needed, in the prime minister's absence.

One of the UK's most famous prime ministers was Winston Churchill.

UNDERSTANDING BETTER

A PRIME MINISTER'S WORK

The role of prime minister is a very important one. The person in this role leads the country through good and bad times. In 2013, former British prime minister Margaret Thatcher died. Read the following *Wall Street Journal* quote about her:

"Mrs. Thatcher is remembered within Britain mostly for her role in revolutionizing the fading economy, in a process that caused huge social change and division, and for the successful retaking of the Falkland Islands, the British South Atlantic territory invaded by Argentina in 1982—after which she declared, 'We have ceased to be a nation in retreat.' In Europe, she is remembered as a prickly leader who thrived on confrontation, but who ultimately agreed to foster some of the European Union's most significant developments…"

After reading this quote, what have you learned about the role of prime minister? What have you learned about the former prime minister Margaret Thatcher?

British prime minister Margaret Thatcher was in office for 11 years.

Legislative Powers

The House of Commons and the House of Lords are the two legislative bodies in the UK parliament. It is typical of a bicameral parliament to have both an upper and lower legislative house.

THE HOUSE OF LORDS

The Lords is the upper house in the UK parliament. Its members are not elected, but are appointed by the monarch, following recommendations from a special committee called the House of Lords Appointments Commission. The prime minister also suggests people for the house. There are three types of members: life peers, bishops, and elected hereditary peers. The peers are the equivalent of the noblemen who originally sat in the Great Council of the medieval period.

THE HOUSE OF COMMONS

The House of Commons is the lower house of the UK parliament. Its members, known as Members of Parliament (MPs), are elected by the people and each represents a certain political party. There can be as many as 10 different parties represented in the house, and each has different values and goals for government.

UK MPs represent one area of the country, such as Amber Rudd for Hastings and Rye.

POLITICAL PARTIES

The three main political parties in the United Kingdom are the Conservatives, Labour, and Liberal Democrats. Generally, two parties dominate parliament. These parties are represented in both the House of Commons and the House of Lords. After an election, the party with the support of the most MPs elected takes control of parliament. This party becomes the majority. The prime minister is chosen from this party. The party in the minority becomes the opposition party. It debates proposals for new laws, known as bills, put forward by the majority party. The opposition party also submits its own bills for consideration by the majority party.

UNDERSTANDING BETTER

THE PARLIAMENTRY CHAMBER

Take a look at the image of the debating chamber at the House of Commons in Canada. It was designed for a two-party system. Notice where the members and speaker sit, and where the public is allowed to sit. Now consider the following: Why do you think the public and the press are allowed to watch the members at work? Why do you think the room was designed this way?

press gallery   speaker   public gallery

majority members   opposition members

Making and Changing Laws

A parliamentary government has to adapt to the needs of its changing country. To make changes, new laws must be created. They are debated in a parliament, where they are called bills. Once passed, these bills become laws. Here is how a bill becomes a law in the UK parliament.

NEW BILLS

First, a government department makes a draft bill. Different committees in the Commons or Lords, or joint committees involving both houses, then review the bill and make changes before it is introduced to parliament. Sometimes, they issue papers about the bills for the public to read and provide responses.

These are usually known as Green Papers, because historically they were printed on green paper to separate them from other types of government documents. Once the draft bill is approved, it can be presented to parliament.

Lords, such as the Rt Honorable Michael Heseltine, pass or decline bills in the House of Lords.

UNDERSTANDING BETTER

THE TIMELINE OF A BILL

This diagram shows the steps a bill takes toward becoming a law in the UK parliament. After reading about how laws are made, what does the diagram tell you that the text does not?

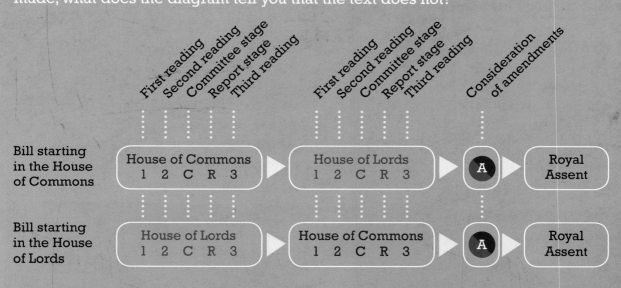

Bill starting in the House of Commons

First reading · Second reading · Committee stage · Report stage · Third reading

House of Commons
1 2 C R 3

First reading · Second reading · Committee stage · Report stage · Third reading

House of Lords
1 2 C R 3

Consideration of amendments

A

Royal Assent

Bill starting in the House of Lords

House of Lords
1 2 C R 3

House of Commons
1 2 C R 3

A

Royal Assent

PRESENTING BILLS

A bill is presented to parliament by the government, an MP or Lord, or a private individual or organization. It can either be presented before the House of Commons or the House of Lords. Once presented, the bill can then be debated. After it is examined and discussed, changes, or amendments, can be made. The House of Commons and the House of Lords both need to agree on the bill's content. Then the amended bill is sent to the monarch.

ROYAL ASSENT

The monarch must give his or her approval. This is called Royal Assent. Once a bill has the Royal Assent, it becomes an Act of Parliament and is a law. The law can then be put into effect by the relevant government department. For example, a law about roads would be the responsibility of the Department of Transport. If a law needs to be changed later, another Act has to be passed before that can happen.

Elections and Voting

In any democratic system, the core value is that the people are involved with the government of their country. People of different areas, called constituencies, choose who represents them in the government. Those elected officials then represent the desires and needs of the people in their constituency.

ELECTING MPS

In the UK parliament, the House of Commons is the elected body of the government, and MPs are the elected representatives. Every five years, the House of Commons is dissolved. This means that every seat becomes vacant and a new House of Commons must be formed. To fill the seats, elections are held throughout the country. If an MP retires, or dies, a single election, called a by-election, takes place in that constituency to find a new representative for that area.

Election papers were counted during the 2010 general election in the United Kingdom.

28

Knesset Hall is home to Israel's parliament.

CONSTITUENCY REPRESENTATIVES

Each voter has a choice of candidates for his or her constituency. The candidates come from different political parties or run as an independent, meaning they do not belong to any party. All candidates have to pay a fee, called a deposit, to take part, which is then returned to them if they receive more than 5 percent of the votes. The candidate who receives the most votes becomes the MP for that constituency. In the House of Commons, the political party that has the most MPs takes control of the house.

In the United Kingdom, there are 650 constituencies, each represented in the House of Commons. There is an average of 68,175 voters in each constituency. Each constituency is represented in the House of Commons.

UNDERSTANDING BETTER

ISRAEL'S HYBRID SYSTEM

Israel has a long history of political struggles. After Israeli prime minister Yitzhak Rabin was assassinated in 1995, a new law was passed that allowed the prime minister to be directly elected by the people. The result was a kind of hybrid parliament, with elements of the presidential system. This elected minister still relies heavily on the support of the parliament, though. Why do you think Israel changed to an elected prime minister? Do you see any problems or advantages in this hybrid system?

Ceremonies and Traditions

Some of the more colorful parts of the UK parliament are its ceremonies and traditions. When the Queen opens a new session of parliament, she wears silks, furs, and a jewel-encrusted crown. The royal carriages and horses carry her from Buckingham Palace to the Houses of Parliament. This is the pomp and ceremony of parliament and some of its traditions date back many centuries.

STATE VISITS

When a leader from another country comes to the United Kingdom to formally represent the interests of their country, this is called a State Visit. This leader will meet the Queen, who entertains them at a State Banquet, and sometimes makes a speech before both Houses of Parliament during the visit. In 2012, Aung San Suu Kyi, a political leader and Nobel Prize winner from Burma, made a speech, and so did US president Barack Obama when he visited the country in 2011.

A coach driver takes Queen Beatrix to the opening of the Dutch parliament in 2010.

STATE OPENING OF PARLIAMENT

The ceremony that gets the most attention is the State Opening of Parliament. It starts the session of parliament for the year. It is the Queen's duty to open the session. She travels from her home in Buckingham Palace to Westminster Palace in a horse-drawn carriage. Huge crowds gather to watch and television crews broadcast the event to the world.

The ceremony takes place in the House of Lords, where the queen sits on her throne. Then the members of the House of Commons are summoned to the event. The Queen then delivers a speech to the two houses. It outlines parliament's goals and plans for the year. This speech is just ceremonial, however. The government writes and approves the points of the speech before the ceremony. While the opening of parliament is symbolic only, it displays some of the more exciting and dramatic aspects of the UK government.

UNDERSTANDING BETTER

THE IMPORTANCE OF MEETING TOGETHER

This image shows the Queen arriving at the State Opening of Parliament. This event is the only time each year that the Queen, the House of Lords, and the House of Commons all meet. The ceremony originates in times when parliament and the monarch did not get along. After reading this information and studying the image, why do you think this ceremony is held each year? What is its importance?

CHAPTER THREE

Living with Parliaments

On Canada Day, thousands of Canadians visit Parliament Hill, in Ottawa, to celebrate the country's birthday on July 1. They wear red and white, like the colors of the country's flag. Ceremonies and performances fill the day, and the celebration ends with fireworks. This is a day of the year that Canadians show their national pride.

Canada Day is celebrated with parades in towns and cities across Canada.

WORKING WITH GOVERNMENT

Life in a country with a parliamentary government involves the people of the country. Their votes decide who runs their country. To best represent the people, a country's residents must be involved with their political system.

In Canada's 2011 general election, 61 percent of the people voted. Other countries with parliamentary systems have higher turnouts, however. Norway gets around 77 percent of its voters to participate in elections. Around 74 percent of New Zealand's people voted in 2011.

SAYING WHAT YOU THINK

It is important in a parliamentary system that people express their opinions. A vote expresses a resident's opinion and directly affects what bills will be supported in a parliament. In turn, the laws that pass then directly affect residents of a country. Residents are not always happy about the laws that are passed by a parliament. If a constituency is unhappy about a new law, its people can express that opinion to their representative. The representative can then try to affect change in parliament on their behalf.

The Maori people lived in New Zealand long before Europeans arrived.

UNDERSTANDING BETTER

ISSUES WITH NEW LAWS

A recent law in New Zealand upset the Maori, the native people of New Zealand. It made the coastline public property, which, until then, had been under the control of the Maori. Here is an excerpt from a *Taipei Times* news story about the issue:

"Prime minister Michael Cullen told parliament the law was about the government 'asserting clear ownership' of the 18,700 km coastal strip on behalf of all New Zealanders. 'There will be disappointment among Maori at the passing of this bill,' but they 'do not own the [coastline] and seabed,' he said.

The law nationalizing New Zealand's coastline passed …after 18 months of anger vented by opponents, who say the move steals land from the Maori. In May, more than 20,000 protesters marched to parliament to denounce the legislation. Some tribes say the new law will block their plans to set up [fish farms] along parts of the coast."

This excerpt shows two sides of an issue. Examine the excerpt. Then, decide what it tells you about New Zealand's parliamentary system.

Media and Parliaments

Access to information and openness are key aspects of parliamentary governments. They are held accountable to the people of their countries. Most parliamentary chambers have public galleries where people can watch debates take place. Otherwise, they can find out what is going on in a parliament from traditional media, such as newspapers and television, or from the Internet.

KNOWING ABOUT BILLS AND DEBATES

In many countries, bills are publicly posted for all to read before a vote is taken. Debates of bills may be videotaped and then posted online. And vote counts are published, too. Knowing what a government is doing is very important in democratic countries. It keeps the people involved with representatives and the decisions that they make.

Russian journalists watched a state council meeting online in April 2012.

INDEPENDENT MEDIA

The media is one method of getting that information out to the people. In parliamentary countries, the government does not control the media. Unlike some countries, such as those run by a dictatorship, where the leaders will limit what the public can find out, in parliamentary countries the government does not control the media. Instead, the media independently reports on the news of the government. Traditionally, the news of the government has been reported through television, newspapers, and websites. Today, social media is changing the way news is reported to the people.

RISE OF SOCIAL MEDIA

In recent years, people have been able to get almost instant access to the news through social media. People in different countries want to have this direct access to their government. A few countries have issued formal policies on how government should use social media, such as Twitter and Facebook. The Canadian government encourages departments to use social media. The UK parliament suggests that members should use Twitter to respond to the public's policy questions. With all forms of media, parliaments today aim to accurately and openly share the news of the government.

UNDERSTANDING BETTER

PARLIAMENT AND TWITTER

Here is a posting from the UK parliament's Twitter account:

@UK Parliament 5 Jun:

Olympic and Paralympic officials give evidence on legacy to Lords Committee at 11a.m.

What does this posting tell you about how the UK parliament uses social media to inform the public?

Social media provides easy access to citizens who want to learn more about the daily activities of their government.

CHAPTER FOUR

Benefits and Issues

Crimes against women are common in India. In 2013, the people were angry that law enforcement was doing nothing to prevent those crimes. Thousands of people protested, and India's parliament responded. A bill passed quickly that imposed tougher penalties against attackers. In a *New York Times* article, Meenakshi Ganguly, the director of Human Rights Watch in South Asia, said, "It is good that India still responds as a democracy when there is pressure from citizens."

QUICK PASSAGE OF LAWS

A benefit of the parliamentary system is that it can quickly pass bills into laws. This is because the executive (governing) powers and the legislative (law-making) powers are fused together. They work together as one voice speaking for the people. This is unlike the presidential system, where the executive and legislative bodies are separate. They do not always have the same opinion, adding conflict and delaying the passage of certain bills.

This group of Indian people protested to voice their opinions, something that citizens have a right to do in democratic countries.

The World Bank suggests that a parliamentary system is one of the most effective forms of government.

LESS CORRUPTION

Throughout history, there are many governments and leaders who have abused their power. Corruption is a huge problem. Some leaders use their powers in government for personal gains. They may, perhaps, steal funds meant to help the people. They may take bribes to pass bills that may not be in the best interest of the public. A recent report by the World Bank, an organization set up in 1944 to help developing countries, studied corruption and political systems. It found that parliaments and democracies have fewer instances of corruption than other types of government.

UNDERSTANDING BETTER

IS A PARLIAMENTARY SYSTEM BETTER?

In the United States, decisions about the budget could not be made in the House of Representatives and the Senate. Here is what CNN reporter Fareed Zakaria had to say about the debate:

"Given this situation, it becomes very easy in a presidential system for the executive and the legislature to get into a classic standoff over benefits as we saw in the debt crisis.

Remember, the political battle surrounding the debt ceiling is actually impossible in a parliamentary system because the executive controls the legislature. There could not be a public spectacle of the two branches of government squabbling and holding the country hostage."

What do you think the author was trying to say about the benefits of a parliamentary government?

Issues with Parliaments

In the parliamentary system, voters cannot directly choose a prime minister, who is the chief executive. Some think this is the main difficulty with a parliamentary system, as the person who is the head of government is not directly accountable to a country's people. This is unlike the system in the United States, where the people must vote their head of government, the president, into office.

THE LACK OF CHECKS AND BALANCES

With the presidential system, there are more checks and balances in the legislative (law-making) process. This means that bills are examined separately by legislative and executive powers. If the house, senate, or executive powers do not agree with a bill, it most likely will not pass. In the parliamentary system, if the majority party wants a bill to pass, it will pass. The exception is when certain members of that party disagree with a proposed law and vote against the government.

This Indian activist protested against government corruption.

UNDERSTANDING BETTER

ITALIAN PARLIAMENT: AN AUTHOR'S VIEWPOINT

In a *New York Times* article, journalist Elisabetta Povoledo wrote:

"In the vote Friday for the speakers of the senate and the lower house, most law-makers cast blank ballots, signaling the inability to find a compromise over the candidates. The parties will try to vote again Saturday, but the strategy underscored the current deadlock in parliament."

What point was the author making about the Italian parliament?

NEED FOR CHANGE

Some countries believe their parliaments need to do things differently. There are Indians who want change in their parliament. Some believe that its members are power hungry and do not represent the needs of the people. The Indian parliament has a reputation for corruption and many Indians are unhappy with their government as a result. Italy's parliament has also had some problems. In 2013, at the start of the first parliamentary session after a general election, neither of the two houses could agree on leaders. Without leaders, no other government business could be done. These are just a few of the issues facing parliamentary systems.

In 2013, Italian lawmakers finally agreed to reelect Giorgio Napolitano as president for a second term.

CHAPTER FIVE

Future of Parliaments

Parliamentary systems of government are spreading. When countries decide to become democracies and need to form new governments, many are choosing a parliamentary system. These parliaments run into similar issues around the world.

NEW PARLIAMENTS

Several countries have recently adopted governments with parliamentary executives. Burma in Southeast Asia changed to a parliamentary system in January 2011. Tunisia also established its parliament in 2011, and began to draft a new constitution. This north African country is a republic with a unicameral (single assembly) legislature.

PARLIAMENTS ACTING TOGETHER

The Inter-Parliamentary Union (IPU) is an organization, founded in 1889, that links these different parliaments together. Its members are made up of more than 160 national parliaments, including the United Kingdom, Germany, Japan, Pakistan, Uganda, Sierra Leone, Venezuela, and Finland.

The IPU sets standards for world parliaments. It provides assistance to new parliaments. It helps countries emerging from conflicts to set up new democratic systems. It serves as a place where members of parliaments can meet and discuss issues within their government systems. The IPU works to

Tunisian protestors fought for a democratic government from 2010 to 2011.

Masai women and children sing traditional songs in Kenya, a country that is considering changing to a parliamentary government.

promote democracy, peace, sustainable development, human rights, women in politics, and education, science, and culture. It also tracks parliaments and their elections around the world.

GOVERNMENTS TOGETHER

As the world becomes increasingly connected, the IPU union helps governments work together to solve world problems. Knowing how one parliament has dealt with an issue may help another country to deal with similar issues.

UNDERSTANDING BETTER

SWITCHING TO A PARLIAMENT

Some countries are considering a switch from a presidential system to a parliamentary system. Former prime minister of Kenya, Raila Odinga, urged in a 2013 news article:

"We need parliamentary democracy where the party with a majority of MPs forms the government. It is the only way through which a person from a small community, like the Maasai or Samburu, can ascend to power. It is a system which has worked very well in mature democracies all over the world."

What reasons does prime minister Odinga give for making a switch to the parliamentary system?

Women in Parliaments

Women have a bright future in parliaments. An IPU study found that the number of women in parliaments worldwide is increasing. In 2013, women took just over 20 percent of parliamentary seats. There were more women in the lower houses of parliaments than in the upper houses. The country with the highest percentage of women in parliament was Rwanda, in Africa, where women held 56 percent of the seats in the country's lower house.

GETTING MORE WOMEN INTO PARLIAMENTS

To work for greater equality between men and women, female members of the parliament in Macedonia, a country in southeastern Europe, started the Women's Parliamentarians' Club in 2003. The club worked to change the law about the inclusion of women candidates in elections. It succeeded, and the new law stated that 30 percent of election candidates from each party had to be women. After the law was passed, 36 women were elected to the country's parliament in 2006. The club continues to work for women's rights by encouraging the passing of more new laws to help women.

A woman casts her vote in the 2011 Spanish general elections.

GREAT FEMALE LEADERS

Many women have also been great leaders of parliaments. Margaret Thatcher was the first and only female prime minister in the UK parliament. She held that position between 1979 and 1990, making her the longest-serving British prime minister of the twentieth century. Indira Gandhi was India's prime minister for more than 11 years, from 1966 to 1977, and then again from 1980 until she was assassinated in 1984. Julia Gillard became the first female Australian prime minister in Australia, serving from 2010 to 2013.

Australian prime minister Julia Gillard greeted Pakistani prime minister Syed Yousuf Raza Gilani on October 28, 2011, in Perth, Australia.

As more women serve in parliaments, they become better systems of government. With women involved, parliaments more equally represent the people of the countries they serve.

UNDERSTANDING BETTER

CHARTING THE NUMBERS OF WOMEN

Take a look at this chart. It shows the ten countries with the highest percentages of women filling their parliamentary seats. What does this chart tell you that the text does not?

Rank	Country	Lower or Single House				Upper House or Senate			
		Elections	Seats	Women	% W	Elections	Seats	Women	% W
1	Rwanda	9 2008	80	45	56.3	9 2011	26	10	38.5
2	Andorra	4 2011	28	14	50	—	—	—	—
3	Cuba	1 2008	586	265	45.2	—	—	—	—
4	Sweden	9 2010	349	156	44.7	—	—	—	—
5	Seychelles	9 2011	32	14	43.8	—	—	—	—
6	Senegal	7 2012	150	64	42.7	—	—	—	—
7	Finland	4 2011	200	85	42.5	—	—	—	—
8	South Africa	4 2009	400	169	42.3	4 2009	53	17	32.1
9	Nicaragua	11 2011	92	37	40.2	—	—	—	—
10	Iceland	4 2009	63	25	39.7	—	—	—	—

What Have You Learned?

The parliamentary system has been around for centuries. This old form of government still thrives today in countries around the world. It is a democratic government that works only if the people of the country are involved. Through elections, representatives become members of parliament. They then represent the voters in their constituencies.

UNDERSTANDING PARLIAMENTARY SYSTEMS

We have seen that a parliamentary system can be either a constitutional monarchy or a republic. If it is a constitutional monarchy, a monarch is the head of state. If it is a republic, a president is the head of state. The heads of state for both types of systems are ceremonial and usually do not have any political powers. The head of government in parliaments is chosen from the majority political party in the assembly. This person is responsible to, and dependent upon, the support of parliament.

The UK parliament continues to make new laws that will shape the country's future.

WHAT ABOUT THE FUTURE?

Parliaments are known for their quick passage of bills into laws. They also work readily with new media such as Twitter to share the information about their legislative work. Women are also an increasing presence in parliaments. With a union of world parliaments, information and assistance is shared with both developing and more experienced parliaments. This old governmental system has adapted to a changing world. It is a political system that is sure to endure into the future.

UNDERSTANDING BETTER

AN IDEAL PARLIAMENT

Edmund Burke was an Irish-born member of the UK parliament in the late eighteenth century. He warned against the corruption of parliaments, stating in 1774:

"Parliament is not a congress of ambassadors from different and hostile interests; which interests each must maintain, as an agent and advocate, against other agents and advocates; but parliament is a deliberative assembly of one nation, with one interest, that of the whole; where, not local purposes, not local prejudices, ought to guide, but the general good, resulting from the general reason of the whole."

What do you think Burke meant by this statement? Do you agree or disagree with his philosophy? From what you have learned, do you think this is how parliamentary government actually works?

Edmund Burke spoke out about the purpose of parliament in the late 1700s.

GLOSSARY

Act a bill that has been passed by the legislature

affirmation the action of stating something as a fact

assembly a group of people who have been elected to make a country's laws

bicameral having two branches

bill a written plan for a new law

cabinet a group of advisors for the head of a country's government

ceremonial a role involving little to no actual power

ceremony the formal actions carried out on an important occasion

colonies territories that have been settled by people from another country

Commonwealth an association that includes the United Kingdom and countries or states that were once part of the British Empire; the British monarch is the head of state for members of the Commonwealth

constituency a group of voters in an area that elects a representative for a legislative body

constitution a set of rules and principles that lays down how a nation should be governed

constitutional monarchy a monarchy where the power of the monarch is limited by a constitution

democracy a system in which the government is voted for by most or all of the adults in that country

dissolved to close down or dismiss

election the process of selecting someone or deciding something by voting

executive the branch of government that creates policy and carries it out

judiciary the branch of government consisting of the judges and law courts

legislative having the power to make laws for a country

legislature the branch of government that debates policy and makes laws

majority the greater number

media the newspapers, radio, television, and other forms of communication

minister a person who is elected to help govern a country

minority the lesser number

monarchy rule by a king or queen, who usually inherits their role

opposition a group that resists the majority

peer a member of the nobility, or a bishop, in the United Kingdom who has a seat in the House of Lords

political party a group of people with similar ideas about how a country should be run

pomp ceremony and magnificent display

representative a person chosen to act on behalf of a larger group

republic a democracy where the head of state is also elected, rather than a hereditary monarch

symbolic serving as a symbol of something

unicameral having a single legislative house

vacant a position that is not filled

FOR MORE INFORMATION

BOOKS

Pratt, Mary K. *Parliaments*. Edina, MN: ABDO, 2011.

Stites, Bill. *Democracy*. New York, NY: Rosen Publishing, 2005.

Summers, Kimberly Dillon. *United Kingdom*. Edina, MN: ABDO, 2012.

Witmer, Scott. *Political Systems*. North Mankato, MN: Heinemann Library, 2012.

WEBSITES

Explore the parliamentary system in Canada at:
parl.gc.ca/About/Parliament/Education/OurCountryOurParliament/home-e.aspx

Learn more about the UK parliament through 1,000 years of British history at:
assets.parliament.uk/education/houses-of-history/main.html#

See how the parliamentary system in Australia works at:
peo.gov.au/kidsview/menu.html

Get an overview of the UK parliament at:
parliament.uk/education/online-resources/videos2/youve-got-the-power/ygtp-parliament-overview

INDEX